Bear Mountain & Harriman State Parks

Arthur's Falls, Beech Trail, May 22

Queensboro Brook, Seven Lakes Drive, October 26

Bear Mountain & Harriman State Parks

NICK ZUNGOLI

Exposures Gallery Press

CONTENTS

7   Bear Mountain & Harriman Parks Map

9   Introduction - Where Nature Meets the City

14   North Section - Trail Map & Photographs

60   Central Section - Trail Map & Photographs

114   South Section - Trail Map & Photographs

156   Hiking & Camping

159   Photography

160   Staying & Eating

163   Arriving - Train, Bus & Car

Left: Forest Dogwood, Long Mountain, May 2

𝒯his book is dedicated to all those who
protect, preserve and cherish the Park.

"The reason to preserve wilderness is that we need it. We need wilderness of all kinds, large and small, public and private. We need to go now and again to places where our work is disallowed, where our hopes and plans have no standing."

Constitution Marsh, Hudson River, Bear Mountain & Highlands, October 16

Although every attempt has been made to ensure accuracy of information contained within this book, the author and publisher do not assume and disclaim any liability to any party for any loss or damage caused by errors or omissions. If the rigors and threats of nature are in any way beyond your capabilities, do not attempt any hike in this guide. Maps in this book are based on 2015 data from the NYSOPRHP GIS Bureau, however serious hikers should supplement their outings with detailed maps made available through the NY/NJ Trail Conference.

First published in the United States of America in 2018
by Exposures Gallery Press, P.O. Box 5, Sugar Loaf, New York 10981
www.exposures.com

© 2018 Nick Zungoli
Quotation credits: Wendell Berry, Chief Seattle, Henry Crow Dog.

All rights reserved. No part of this publication may be reproduced, stored in a retrrieval system, or transmitted in any form or by any means, electronic, mechanical, photocopying, recording, or otherwise, without prior consent of the publisher.

Printed in China

ISBN: 13: 978-0-9755732-1-1 | Library of Congress Control Number: 2018905364

Bear Mountain & Harriman Parks

The Park is one hour from New York City by car or train.

Where Nature Meets the City

For almost 40 years, I have gone here, like a pilgrim, to renew my contact with nature and feed my need for beauty and wonder. It is as important and interesting to me now as it was new then. This book is my way of sharing that with you.

I arrived in the Hudson Valley's little hamlet of Sugar Loaf in 1979. As a nature and travel photographer I was immediately captivated by the wealth of subject matter the "Park" offered right at my doorstep. Thirty miles from the streets of New York City, there are fifty thousand acres of wild nature in Harriman and Bear Mountain State Parks. Amazing! This book can help you discover and enjoy the year-round beauty that has been an important part of my personal and professional life over the years. I have identified the images in this book by the exact place in the Park and day of the year to help you begin to experience the Park as I have. At the end of the book, I've included information on what I've learned about getting to the parts of the Park, hiking, camping, making photographs and other useful visitor information.

There seem to be three good ways to ease into the overwhelming size of the Park. First, just drive around; Second, the Trailside Museums and the Bear Mountain Inn are interesting and informative destinations; Third, just grab your pack, lace up your boots and explore. The place names in the Park are doorways into the history and mystery of the Park. Pick a few to find your way to Reeves Meadow and Stony Brook, The Timp, The Tornes, Lemon Squeeze, Island Pond, Almost Perpendicular or Hippo Rock.

Discover the Park along Seven Lakes Drive, the main road which bisects the Park and extends for just under 18 miles south to north. Starting from the village of Sloatsburg, the scenic drive passes Lake Sebago; Lake Kanawauke; Lake Skannatati and Lake Askoti; Lake Tiorati; Silver Mine Lake and finally, the seventh, Queensboro Lake. The Bear Mountain Bridge at the northern gateway into the park affords grand views of the Hudson River and the Highlands. It was here that the first section of the 2100-mile long Appalchian Trail was opened in 1923. Perkins Memorial Drive also is not be missed. It reaches the summit of Bear Mountain where Perkins Tower provides a view of four states and the Manhattan skyline.

November 30 to April 1, Perkins Drive, Route 106, Lake Welsh Parkway and Arden Valley Road connecting to Tiorati Brook Drive are all closed. Year-round roadside parking is limited to designated areas only.

Left: West Facing Rock, Breakneck Mountain, October 12

The Park incorporates early native sites and a few Revolutionary War places. Before taking to the trails, deepen the understanding of your experience by visiting the various park museums. Forts Montgomery and Clinton played a prominent role during the American Revolution. Control of the Hudson River was essential and the area that was to become the park saw significant military engagements. A great chain crossed and blockaided the river, forged from local iron-ore mines. Although filled in, many of the mines can still be found. At the Fort Montgomery State Historic Site visitors can tour the remains of the 14-acre fortification, perched on a cliff overlooking the Hudson. A foot bridge across the Popolopen Brook connects both forts.

At the nearby Trailside Museums and Zoo, visit local injured or rehabilitating animals, including bears, otters, deer, bald eagles, and owls. The Reptile and Amphibian House has many species of fish, turtles, snakes and frogs. The Nature Study, Geology, Colonial and Native American History Museums are also located in the complex. Iona Island Bird Sanctuary is on the parks eastern edge in the Hudson River within the Northeastern coastal forests ecoregion. Bald eagles have rookeries here and are frequently spotted fishing the open waters.

Dawn, Bear Mountain Bridge, Hudson River and Popolopen Brook, October 4

Upscale accommodations and dining can be found at The Bear Mountain Inn. Originally completed in 1915, it is an early example of the rustic lodge style influenced by the Adirondack Great Camps and later used extensively in the National Park System. Along with the Inn, Overlook Lodge and Stone Cottages are located beside Hessian Lake. There are facilities here to boat, swim, sled and ice skate.

Seasonal rustic camps are found at the Lake Sebago Cabins and at Beaver Pond Campground where tent and trailer sites are available. The Appalachian Mountain Club has an outdoor center open to the public on Breakneck Pond with cabins and tent platforms. There are many other group camps throughout the park run by not-for-profit organizations as well. An adventurous way to spend an overnight is backpacking to and camping at a lean-to shelter. There are nine of them scattered about Harriman Park. Officially, they are the only locations in the park besides the designated campgrounds where overnight camping is allowed. No reservations are required for these shelters as they operate on a first-come, first-served basis.

Picnicking is only permitted in designated areas in the Park. Ground fires, tents and hammocks are prohibited.

The "Park" was created through a collection of early 20th century negotiations and land deals on October 29, 1910, when Edward Harriman's son Averell presented a deed for 10,000 acres of land and a million-dollar check to the Palisades Park Commission. As part of the agreement with the Harriman family, New York did away with a plan to build a prison along the Popolopen Brook and appropriated an additional $2.5 million to acquire additional land and construct park facilities. Another $1.5 million came from private subscription, while New Jersey contributed an amount deemed reasonable by the Commission.

Today Harriman and Bear Mountain Parks 50,000 plus acres are at the core of a contiguous protected forest in the New York and New Jersey Highlands. It contains over 300 miles of marked trails and wood roads, thirty-six lakes, numerous streams and mountain vistas and links the 18,000 acre Sterling Forest State Park to the south with the United States Military Academy's 16,000-acre forest reserve and Storm King forest reserve of 1,900 acres to the north.

It's been said that a picture is worth a thousand words. My hope is that the photographs in this book will be an inspiration and catalyst to walk in nature and breathe in its beauty - so vital for the human spirit and creativity. At some point over the years of exploring the Park, it became evident that being at the right place and time was critical not only to making compelling images, but also to enjoying its beauty to the fullest. Consider the weather when you go to have a peak experience. Mornings are often softened by the mists that blanket the many lakes and meadows producing a dreamy landscape. Sunny, windless days create mirrior-like lakes that reflect puffy clouds and bright autumn colors. After a storm, clearing skies always create a dramatic sunset or sunrise. The public lands of Bear Mountain and Harriman Parks will by law be preserved forever. "Take only memories and leave only footprints," so that the beauty you experience will remain for future generations to enjoy and cherish.

- NICK ZUNGOLI

Above: Manhattan Skyline from Hawks Cliff, June 20
Right: Snowfall, Seven Lakes Drive, November 28

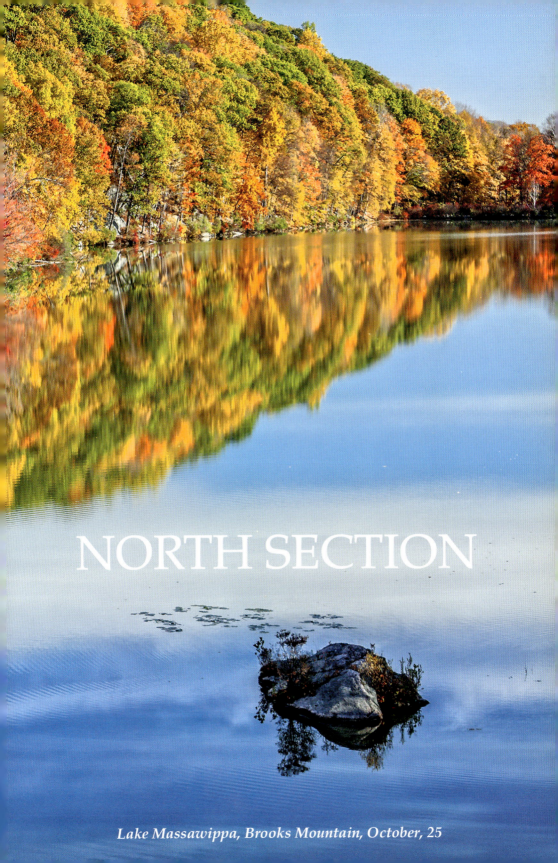

NORTH SECTION MAP

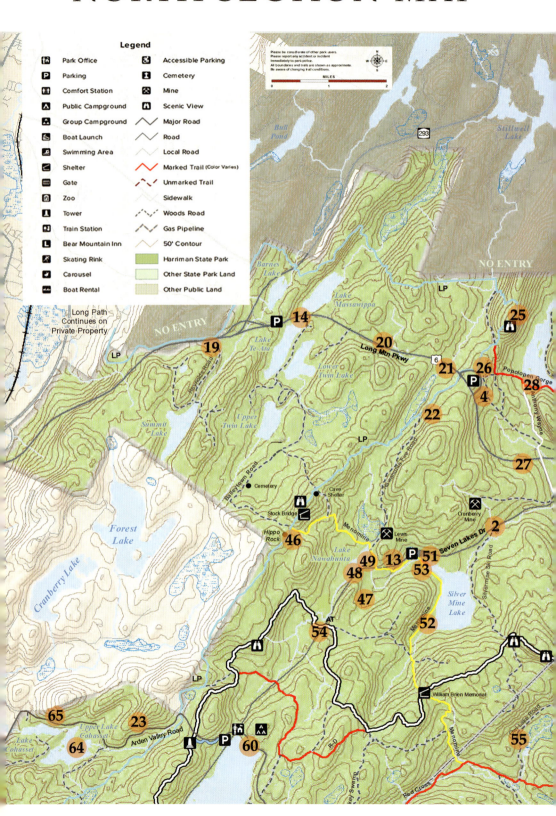

1 The numbers correspond to page numbers in this book.

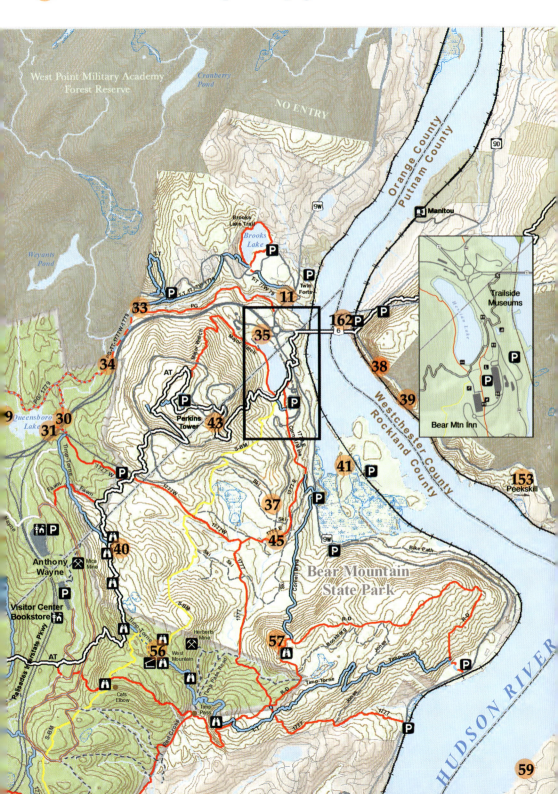

Above: Wetland in Morning Fog, Long Mountain Parkway, November 20
Right: Wetland & Meadow, Long Mountain Parkway, November 5
Preceding Page: Forest Snowfall, Long Mountain Parkway, December 13

Above: Forest Fog, Stockbridge Mountain, December 12
Right: Snake Roots, Lindley Mountain, November 5

Above: Snowy Woods, Long Path, February 23
Right: Crimson Dogwood, Long Mountain Parkway, November 10
Preceding Page: Turkey Hill Lake, October 21

Above: Turkey Hill Lake Reflections, October 19
Right: Bear Mountain View, Queensboro Lake, September 28

Above: Swans and Signets, Queensboro Lake, September 25
Below: Snowy Day, Queensboro Lake, February 12
Left: Fallen Leaves, Queensboro Lake, October 20

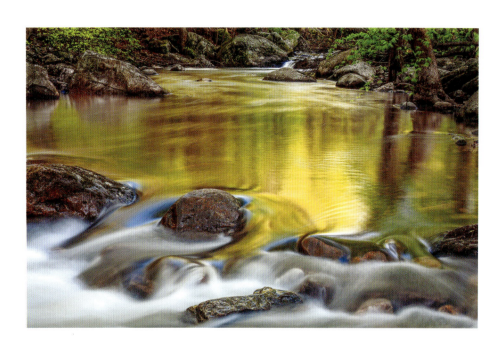

Above: Reflected Spring Colors, Popolopen Brook, May 4
Right: Autumn Bough, Hessein Lake, October 15
Preceding Page: Spring Flow, Popolopen Brook, May 4

Fresh Snow, Hudson River and Iona Island View, February 12

Winter Storm, Bear Mountain Inn view from Route 202, January 9

Morning Mists, Dunderberg Mountain from Route 202, May 16

West Mountain Rainbow and Hudson River View, August 20

Marshland, Iona Island, November 4

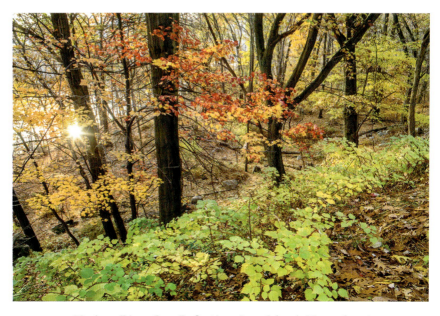

Hudson River Sun Reflection, Iona Island, November 4

First Light, Bear Mountain Bridge and Hudson River from Perkins Drive, October 26

Above: Hippo Rock, Stockbridge Mountain, March 29
Right: Hemlock Grove, Seven Lakes Drive, May 2
Preceding Page: Sunlight, Doodletown Reservoir, June 16

Above: Canadian Geese and Gosslings, Lake Nawahunta, May 2
Below: Wet Snow, Lake Nawahunta, November 28
Left: Fallen Leaves, Lake Nawahunta, October 17

Above: Autumn Reflection & Swamp Maple, Silvermine Lake, November 13
Right: Dawn, Silvermine Lake, October 18
Preceding Page: Autumn Color, Silvermine Lake, October 21

Above: Heart Stump, Owl Swamp Road, May 31
Left: Autumn Color, Seven Lakes Drive, October 15

*Left: The Timp and Hudson River from West Mountain Shelter, November 11
Below: Bear Mountain, Hudson River and Highlands from Bald Mountain, April 25
Following Page: Dusk, Dunderburg and Bear Mountains along the Hudson River, June 29*

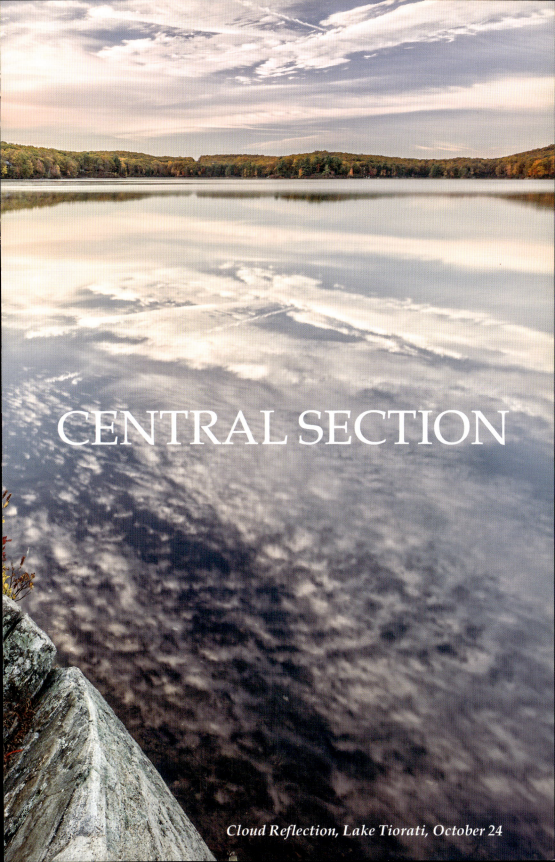
Cloud Reflection, Lake Tiorati, October 24

CENTRAL SECTION MAP

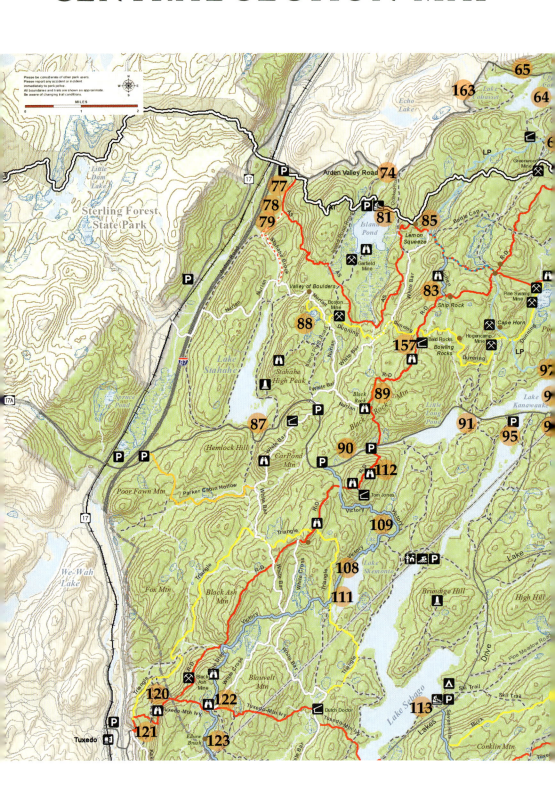

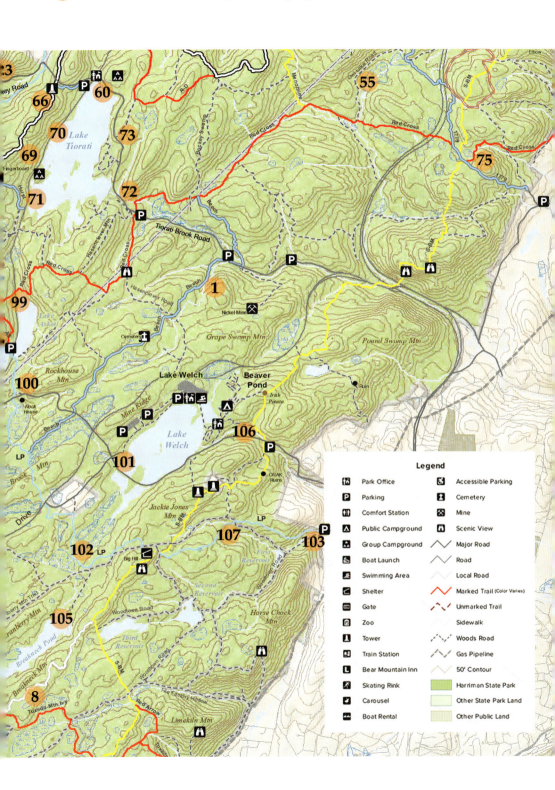

1 The numbers correspond to page numbers in this book.

Above: Lake Cohasset, October 25
Left: Upper Lake Cohasset, October 23

Tripod Rock, Fingerboard Mountain, September 20

Moss & Grass Reflection, Fingerboard Mountain, May 21

Left: Autumn Shore, Lake Tiorati, October 27
Below: Dawn, Lake Tiorati, June 15
Preceding Page: Mountain Laurel and Morning Fog, Fingerboard Mountain, June 11

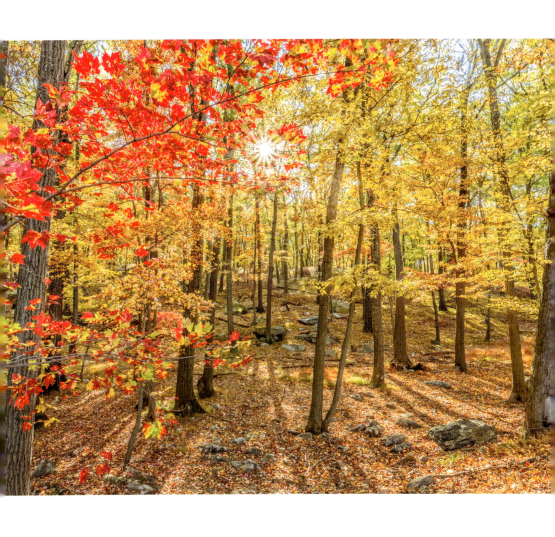

Above: Autumn Woods & Sunlight, Tiorati Brook Road, October 23
Left Top: Tiorati Brook Falls, Red Cross Trail, May 17
Left Bottom: White Tail Doe, Red Cross Trail, May 17

Grass Tussocks, Echo Brook, March 5

Icy Bog, 1779 Trail, February 5

Above: Storm Sky, Elk Pen & Green Pond Mountain, October 12
Left: Heavy Frost, Elk Pen, October 31
Preceding Page: Oak Tree, Elk Pen, October 25

Above: Surebridge Mountain Vista, October 25
Preceding Page: Dusk, Island Pond, October 25

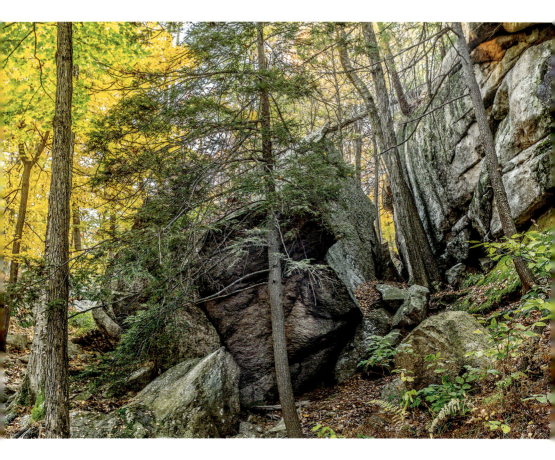

Above & Right: Lemon Squeeze, October 25

Above: Spring Color, Black Mountain, May 1
Left: Autumn Color, Green Pond, October 11
Preceding Page, Autumn Reflections, Lake Stahahe, October 11

Above & Below: Water Lilies, Little Long Pond, June 5
Left: Mountain Laurel, Black Rock Mountain, June 11

Above: White Pines at Sunrise & Turkey Fungus, September 16
Right: Starry Sky, Kanawauke Lake, September 1
Preceding Page, Autumn Colors, Kanawauke Circle, October 24

Above: Storm Front, Lake Skanatati, June 7
Right: Mountain Laurel, Lake Skanatati, June 13

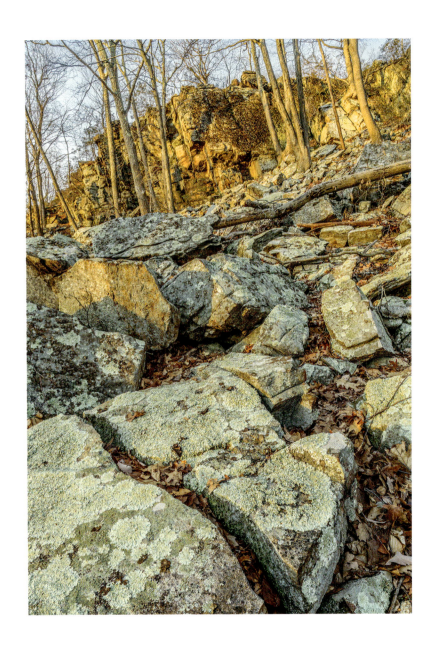

Above: Lake Welsh Thaw, March 13
Left: Lichen Rocks, Rockhouse Mountain, February 12
Preceding Page: Lake Askoti & Frosted Rockhouse Mountain, February 12

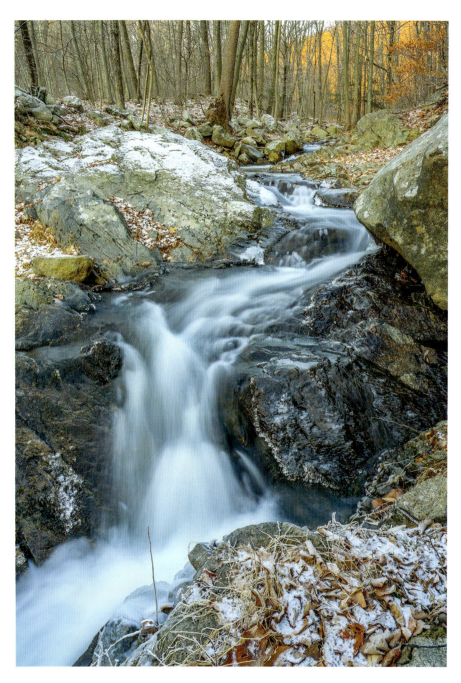

Above: Horse Chock Creek Cascade, February 3
Left: Sundown, Beaver Pond Brook, March 9
Following Page: Morning Sky, Breakneck Pond, October 13

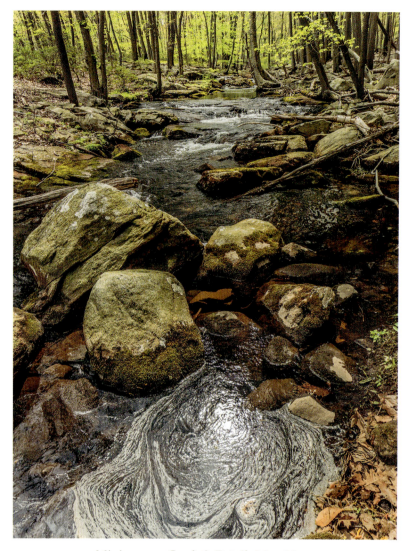

Minisceongo Creek & Detail, May 10

Horse Chock Creek & Detail, March 23

Autumn Color, Lake Skenonto, October 17

Autumn Forest, Victory Trail, October 17

Left: Lake Sebago from Parker Cabin Mountain, March 21
Below: Spring Buds, Lake Sebago, April 24
Preceding Page: Autumn Shore, Lake Skenonto, October 17

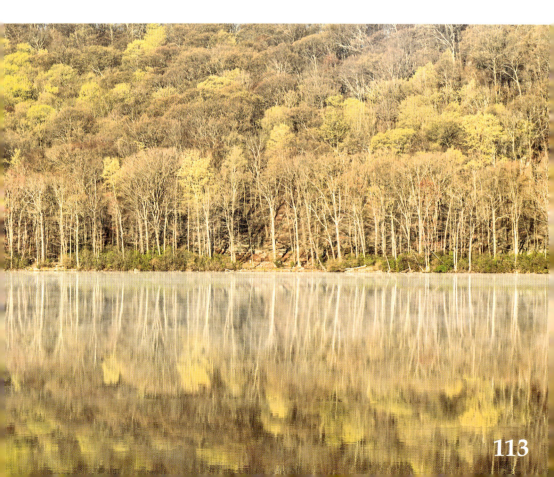

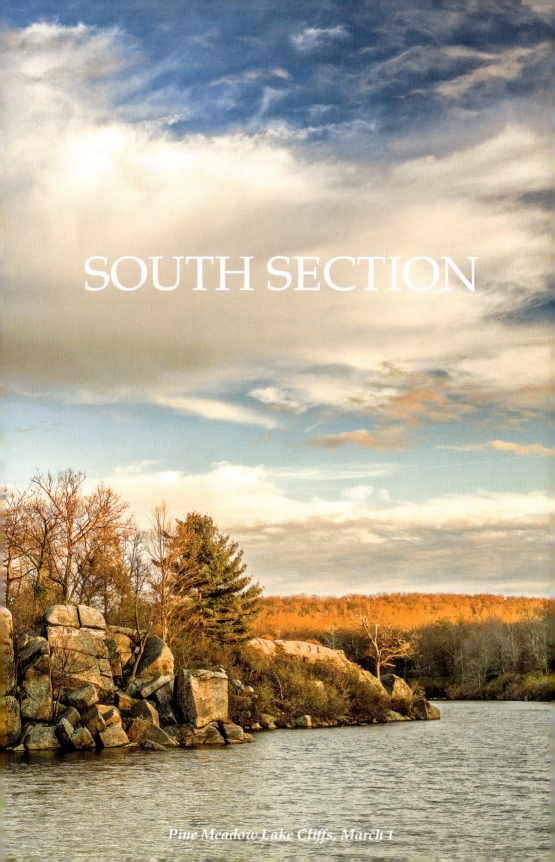

SOUTH SECTION

Pine Meadow Lake Cliffs, March 1

SOUTH SECTION MAP

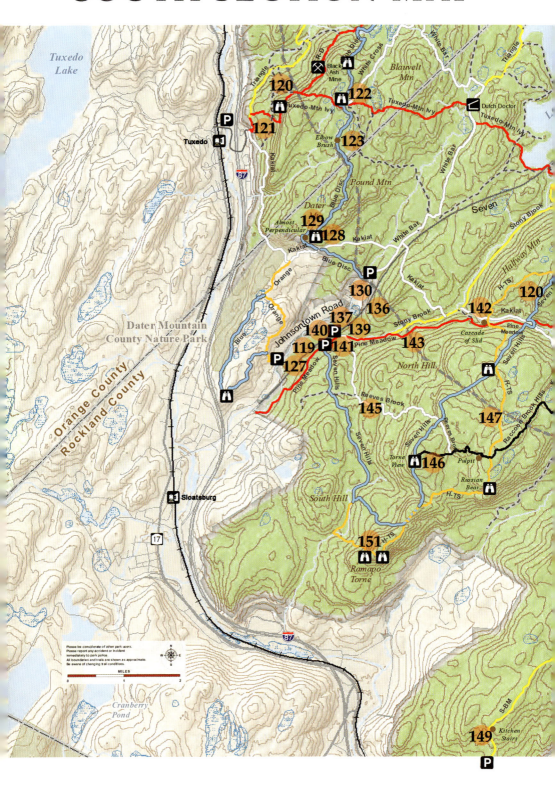

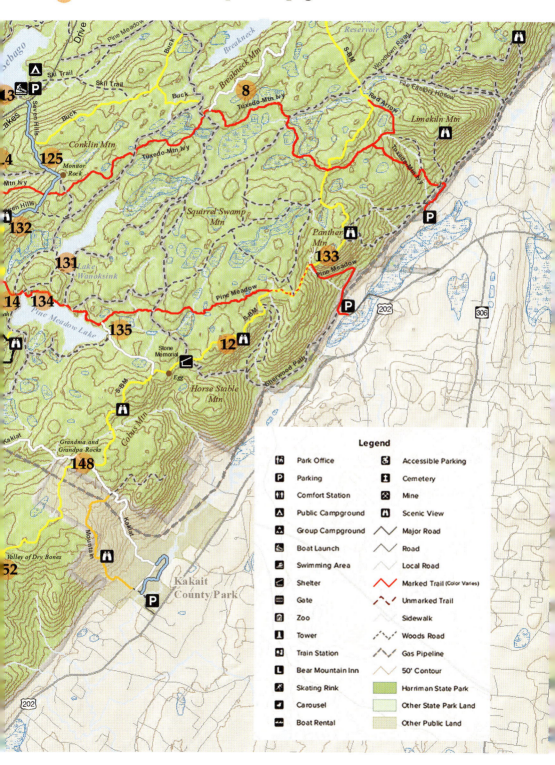

Above: Nor'easter, Pine Hill, March 2
Right: Ramapo-Dunderburg Trail Head, March 2
Preceding Page: Blooming May Apple, Reeves Meadow, May 8

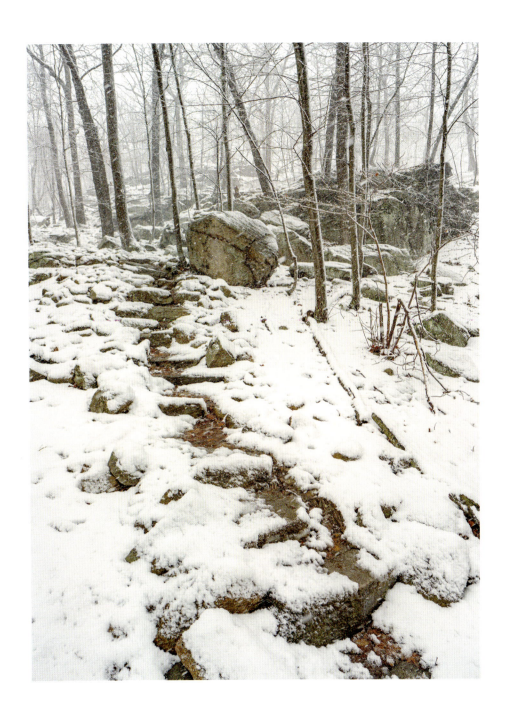

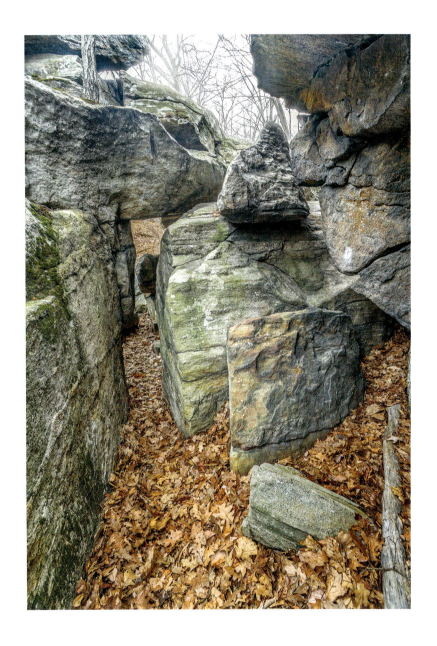

Above: The Elbow Brush, Pound Mountain, March 6
Left: Claudius Smith Den, Blauvelt Mountain, August 30

Above: Forest Shadows, Woodtown Road, March 29
Right: Diamond Creek, Conklin Mountain, March 1

Above: Chipmunk Mountain & Ramapo Torne View, March 8
Top: Clearing Storm, Almost Perpendicular Summit, March 8
Left: Almost Perpendicular Summit, March 6
Preceding Page: Winter View, Almost Perpendicular, January 25

Above: Fresh Snow, Spring Creek, March 3
Right: Lake Wanoksink Thaw, March 1

Glacial Eratic, Diamond Moiuntain, August 24

Glacial Eratic, Panther Mountain, January 18

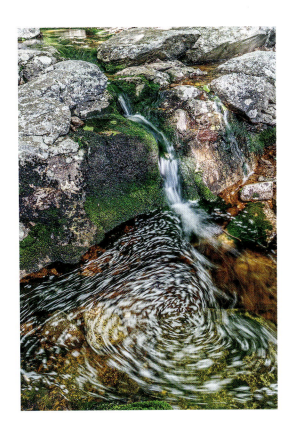

Above: Pine Meadow Brook Details, June 20
Left: Sunrise, Pine Meadow Lake, August 23

Above: Winter Boughs, Seven Lakes Drive, March 8
Right: Spring Boughs & Stony Brook, Seven Lakes Drive, May 5

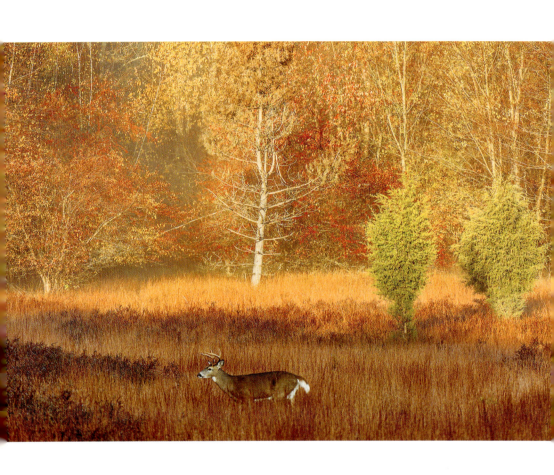

Above: White Tail Buck, Reeves Meadow, October 23
Right: Mossy Rocks & Reflected Color, Reeves Brook, May 5
Preceding Page: Autumn Color, Stony Brook, October 20

Above: Ice Pies, Quartz Brook, January 25
Left: Cascade of Slid, Pine Meadow Brook, August 24
Following Page: Mossy Bog, South Hill, May 6

Above & Below: Rock Lichen, Ramapo Torne, May 3

Grandma & Grandpa Rocks, Cobus Mountain, May 7
Preceding Page: Glacial Deposit, Chipmunk Mountain, October 11

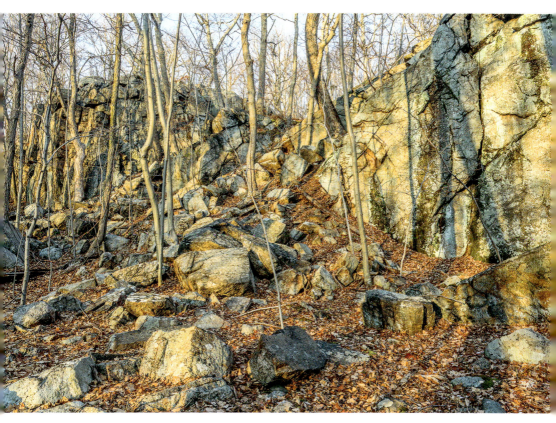

Kitchen Stairs, Nordkop Mountain, January 16
Following Page: Ramapo Torne Vista, May 3

*Above: Hudson River Sunset over Dunderberg and Bear Mountains, August 15
Left: Cascade, Valley of Dry Bones, February 27*

*Following Pages: Left to Right - Cardinal Flower; Garter Snake; Monarch Butterfly;
Blue Flag Iris; Frosted Leaf; Sweet White Violet & Fiddlehead; Orange Cap Mushroom;
Icy Brook; Frozen Leaves; Blue Violet & Shelf Fungus; Autumn Puddle; Green Frog.*

Hiking & Camping

I'd never been camping until a college buddy offered an extra backpack and sleeping bag to me. We walked through fern gully and climbed the mountain up switchbacks that took us past stands of trees with limbs reaching out reminiscent of a Tim Burton film. At the summit I witnessed an orange ball sink into layers of misty ridges. It was transformative and then events took a wrong turn. The temperature dropped and I unfurled my sleeping bag to find it barely reached my armpits. With the zipper rusted solid in the open position, the night seemed without end as I shivered till morning. Somehow I managed to get a fire going with fingers that worked like chopsticks and feet so cold I mistakenly put my shoes on the wrong feet. Yes, I was hooked for life, but never went out unprepared again.

Here is some solid advice. Never walk in the woods without map, water, flashlight and appropriate clothing. When camping, make sure you bring what you need to stay warm and dry. Don't leave a mess behind. It's pretty much that simple.

For me packing is a pleasure, synonymous with the excitement of a new adventure. To make it easy I have lists to refer to for day hikes, overnights or extended walks. Not carrying more weight than you need is the best part of being this organized. That's not to say that you will never be uncomfortable again. Mother nature can be cruel and hand out some unexpected travails, but that's what makes it an adventure. In hind-sight, I will confess that some of my most memorable hikes involved a fair measure of drama. Generally, a good story features pleasure at someone elses expense, sometimes even your own.

So check the weather forecast, pack your bag and tell someone where you're going. No need to fear - hiking is statistically safer than sitting at home in front of the TV. Instead of watching someone else's adventure, make your own. As you go, also consider the amazing work that the volunteer trail builders and maintainers have done to give you safe passage into the wild.

In addition to hiking in the park, mountain biking and cross-country skiing are allowed only at the Anthony Wayne Recreation Area. Fishing is permitted in many of the parks lakes and streams with a New York State fishing license. Non-motorized private boats require a park permit to obtain a key to the launching ramps. Horseback riding, hunting and trapping is not permitted.

For Park information: 845-786-2701; www.palisadesparksconservancy.org
For detailed trail maps: NY/NJ Trail Conference website. www.nynjtc.org

Here's what I carry with me on a day hike: *Camera with wide, normal and zoom telephoto lens (one of these capable of doing macro); Filter kit (extra camera battery, memory card and lens wipes); a tripod that doubles as a hiking staff; Map; cell phone (service in park is poor); flashlight; water bottle; first aid kit; moist wipes; mini towel; plastic bags; multi-tool; lighter; note pad and marker. In warm weather I bring bug repellent, sun screen and chap stick. Clothing includes a hat; bandana; and rainjacket. For cold weather hiking, I add a down vest and mittens. Easy to pack snack foods include: nuts; fruit; cheese and deli meat.*

On an overnight *I'll also pack a rain tarp; small umbrella; sleeping bag and pad; camp stove and cook kit; water filter; food; toiletries and tent (if shelter is not available). I tend not to bring much more than I need to avoid suffering, but everyones comfort level is different.*

Bald Rocks Shelter, May 1

Photography

After a few outings, most people can learn to use a digital camera's settings - however the challange has always been to "find" or "see" a great photo. My best advice is to slow down and use your head and heart before clicking. Fill the frame with your subject while ruthlessly cutting out anything that interferes or distracts. When the light and dark areas that the sun casts in the frame is balanced along with the composition, you'll always have a pretty good photo. Generally, a compelling landscape image starts with finding a beautiful background and then searching for a visually interesting foreground to invite the viewer in. Weather can help to provide the beautiful backdrop - stormy skies, golden light - you'll know it when you see it.

When you find "the shot", here's a quick list to consider:
1 - Have a clear subject and keep out distracting elements.
2 - Don't put the subject in the center - use rule of thirds.
3 - Keep the horizon line straight but not in the center.
4 - Get the focus sharp and camera steady. (a tripod helps)
5 - Create an emotional response with interesting light.

Once I'm ready to shoot, I'll set the camera's quality to **RAW** to produce the best image. Auto settings create JPG's that rely on the camera to auto adjust color, contrast, white balance, sharpening and other important image properties. RAW files give you millions more colors and puts you in creative control of the photo.

Next - I set my camera mode to **Aperture Priority** most often because I can select the F-Stop to creatively control depth-of-field. The camera automatically sets the shutter speed getting you close to the correct exposure quickly. If I'm off the tripod, I'll select a higher ISO for faster shutter speeds to avoid camera movement.

Finally - If the image looks too light or too dark, I adjust the **Exposure Compensation** (+/- button on many cameras) and shoot again. Once you learn to use the histogram in the playback mode you'll have the right exposures all the time.

Probably the best part of digital photography is instantly seeing your image and learning from it. So review, be adventuresome and reshoot till it makes you happy.

With millions of people visiting Bear Mountain and Harriman State Parks we all have a responsibility to minimize our impact. Our zeal to get that special photograph can take us off trail and lead to destruction of plants and animal habitat. Take care to photograph the Park without destroying it.

Left: Stony Brook Fern, June 5

Staying & Eating

BEAR MOUNTAIN INN
A national treasure with 15 deluxe guestrooms and suites built in 1915 of local stone and timber overlooking the shores of Hessian Lake. Fine dining is available at *Restaurant 1915* and the *Blue Roof Tapas Bar*, while quick snacks and picnic lunches are offered at *Hiker's Cafe* and *Stand 10*.

OVERLOOK LODGE
24 standard guestrooms of Overlook Lodge are a hiker's dream or a honeymooner's delight offering rustic comfort. Relax fireside (seasonal) in the lobby, which boasts fabulous panoramic views of the Hudson River.

STONE COTTAGES
4 cottages with 6 individual guestrooms per cottage perfect for anyone looking for an authentic, rustic mountain cabin experience without the expense of renting an entire cabin. Each has a porch and common area with wood-burning fireplace, microwave, mini-refrigerator and dry bar.
845 786 2731; www.visitbearmountain.com

BEAVER POND CAMPGROUND
140 campsites to accomodate tents, trailers and RVs. The A Section has 24 platform sites, some with great views of Lake Welsh. Fishing when seasonally available, swimming and boating (permit required) are offered at Lake Welsh.
845 947 2792; www.reserveamerica.com

SEBAGO CABIN CAMP
39 rustic cabins and two full service cottages in a heavy wooded area on Lake Sebago. Visitors can rent boats, swim, bike, hike and play tennis.
845 351 2360; www.reserveamerica.com

AMC HARRIMAN OUTDOOR CENTER
The Appalachian Mountain Club facility is located on Breakneck Pond. It includes 6 cabins, 3 group lodges, 5 shelters, 12 tent platforms, dining hall and rec meeting hall. Dinner and breakfast are also available to campers in the dining room. Guests can use canoes and kayaks at no charge.
603 466 8059; www.outdoors.org

Above: AMC Outdoor Center at Breakneck Pond
Right: Restaurant 1915 at Bear Mountain Inn

Arriving

TRAIN

Use any of the NJ Transit train lines to Secaucus Junction and then transfer to the Metro-North Port Jervis Line to Suffern or Tuxedo stations. It's one hour of travel time from New York City's Penn Station and then a short walk to the park trail heads when you arrive. The Metro-North Hudson Line from New York City's Grand Central Station to Manitou is another option, but involves a mile hike from the station to the park, including an exhilarating section over the Bear Mountain Bridge. *www.njtransit.com and www.mta.info*

BUS

The Short Line bus from New York City's Port Authority Terminal can drop off at several points along their West Point route including: Suffern, Route 202/Viola Road, Tompkins Cove, Jones Point and Bear Mountain Inn. The Middletown, NY route from Port Authority stops at trail heads in Suffern, Sloatsburg, Tuxedo, Southfields and Arden. *212-736-4700; web.coachusa.com/shortline*

If you arrive in Tuxedo, a seasonal Harriman Park Shuttle Bus is available to drop off riders at trail heads, parking and camp locations on it's route.
www.bettertuxedo.ticketleap.com/tuxedo-harriman-park-shuttle/

CAR

From New York City and points south of the park take the Palisades Parkway or Interstate 287 to NY Route 17 north. From points north of the park take NY Thruway 87 to exit 16 and Routes 6 east or 17 south to park entrances.

The following parkroads are closed November 30 to April 1: Tiorati Brook Road and Lake Welch Drive, Arden Valley Road and County Route 106, from the Kanawauke Circle to Route 17.

Above: Arden Valley Road, October, 20
Left: Metro-North Hudson Line at Manitou, October 28

Above: Harriman Forest Textures, Winter, Spring, Summer, Autumn

"The earth is a living thing. Mountains speak, trees sing, lakes can think, pebbles have a soul, rocks have power."